Minibeasts
In the Compost Heap

Sarah Ridley

A⁺

Smart Apple Media

Smart Apple Media
P.O. Box 3263, Mankato, Minnesota 56002

Printed in the United States

Published by arrangement with the
Watts Publishing Group Ltd, London.

Library of Congress Cataloging-in-Publication Data

Ridley, Sarah.
   In the compost heap / Sarah Ridley.
       p. cm. -- (Where to find minibeasts)
   Includes index.
   Summary: "Profiles many insects and invertebrates
found in compost heaps, discussing their eating
habits, habitats, and survival skills"--Provided by
publisher.
   ISBN 978-1-59920-327-0 (hardcover)
   1. Compost animals--Juvenile literature. 2. Soil
invertebrates--Juvenile literature. 3. Compost--
Juvenile literature. I. Title.
   QL110.5.R53 2010
   592'.1754--dc22

                                          2008045874

Series editor: Sarah Peutrill
Art director: Jonathan Hair
Design: Jane Hawkins
Illustrations: John Alston

9 8 7 6 5 4 3 2 1

The measures for the minibeasts in this book are typical sizes for the type of species shown in the photograph. Different species vary in size.

Picture credits and species guide:
front cover t: Children, Jason Smalley/Alamy. **Front cover b**: May bug (*Melolontha vulgaris*) grub, Fotosav/istockphoto. **2**: Compost heap, Jeff Gynane/Shutterstock. **3**: Earthworms (*Lumbricus terrestris*) in compost, Phil Danze/istockphoto. **6**: Earthworms (*Lumbricus terrestris*), Rosemary Mayer/FLPA Images. **7t**: Children with compost bin, Mike J. Thomas/FLPA Images. **7b**: Planting a shrub, Chris Bernard/istockphoto. **8**: Cultivated apple (*Malus domestica*), Angela Hampton/FLPA Images. **9t**: Compost heap, Jeff Gynane/Shutterstock. **9b**: Slug (*Arion ater*) in compost, Jean-Claude Teyssier. **10t**: Fruit flies (*Drosophila melanogaster*) on compost, Jean-Claude Teyssier. **10b**: Mediterranean fruit fly (*Ceratitis capitata*) larvae on a peach, Nigel Cattlin/FLPA Images. **11**: Common fly (*Musca domestica*) on a pear, Plastique/Shutterstock. **12t**: Garden snail (*Helix aspersa*) near compost heap, Joseph Hoyle/istockphoto. **12b**: Slug (*Arion hortensis*) in compost, Visual Density/ istockphoto. **13t**: Garden snail (*Helix aspersa*), Richard Ford/Digital Wildlife. **13b**: Slug (*arion ater*), Steve McWilliam/Shutterstock. **14tl**: Spider's web, Fotosaw/ Shutterstock. **14tr**: Wolf spider (*Pardosa amentata*) on a compost heap, Jean-Claude Teyssier. **15t**: Centipede (*Lithobius forficatus*), Richard Ford/ Digital Wildlife. **15b**: Blackbird (*Turdus merula*), David Dohnall/Shutterstock. **16t**: Woodlice (*Oniscus asellus*), Nancy Nehring/ istockphoto. **16b**: Pill woodlouse (*Armadillium vulgare*), Richard Ford/Digital Wildlife. **17t**: Black Millipede (*Glomeris marginata*), Richard Ford/Digital Wildlife. **17b**: Common or European Earwig (*Forficula auricularia*), Richard Ford/Digital Wildlife. **18t**: Earthworms (*Lumbricus terrestris*) in compost, Phil Danze/ istockphoto. **18b**: Tiger worm (*Eisenia foetida*), Nigel Cattlin/FLPA Images. **19**: Common earthworn (*Lumbricus terrestris*), Dr Jeremy Burgess/SPL. **20t**: Ground beetle (*Harpalus froelichi*) on compost heap, Richard Becker/FLPA Images. **20b**: Violet ground beetle (*Carabus intricatus*), Mark Moffat/FLPA Images. **21t**: Rose chafer (*Cetonia aurata*) grub, Hecker/Sauer/Still Pictures. **21b**: Rose chafer (*Cetonia aurata*) beetle, Y Xowert/Shutterstock. **22**: Children, Jason Smalley/Alamy. **23t**: False scorpion (*Neobisium carcinoides*), N A Callow/NHPA. **23c**: Velvet mite (*Allothrombium sp.*), N A Callow/NHPA. **23b**: Springtail (*Tomocerus minor*), P. Hartmann/ Still Pictures. **24**: Compost heap, Edward Shaw/ istockphoto. **25t**: Compost heap, David Hosking/ FLPA Images. **25cl**: Compost bin, Gusto Images/SPL. **25cr**: Compost bin, Jeff Gynane/Shutterstock. **25b**: Food scraps, Jenny Home/Shutterstock. **27t**: Compost bin, Jeff Gynane/Shutterstock. **31**: Earthworms (*Lumbricus terrestris*), Rosemary Mayer/FLPA Images.

Contents

Words in **bold** are in the glossary on pages 28–29.

 Adults may want you to wear disposable gloves when you are looking through compost.

Compost Home

Poke around in a compost heap and you will find worms and other minibeasts wriggling around. They are there because there is plenty for them to eat.

▶ Worms eat the fruit and vegetable scraps and dead plants in a compost heap.

What Is a Minibeast?

Minibeast is the name given to thousands of small **animals**, from bees to beetles and worms to woodlice. Although many are **insects**, others are not. None of them have a **backbone**, so scientists give them the name **invertebrate**.

TOP TIP!

Look for boxes like this one throughout the book. They give tips on how to become an ace minibeast spotter.

What Is a Compost Heap?

A compost heap is a pile of dead plant material, vegetable and fruit scraps, newspaper, and even tea bags. It slowly **rots** to form compost. It is an excellent **habitat** for minibeasts. Some eat the plant and vegetable waste while others eat other minibeasts in the heap.

▲ The dark compost at the bottom of the heap is ready to use on the garden.

Why Have a Compost Heap?

Compost helps plants to grow well when it is added to the soil. Making compost also helps to reduce the amount of garbage that people put out for collection.

◀ The nutrients in the compost will be sucked up by this plant's roots.

How Do Compost Heaps Work?

The material in compost heaps turns into compost because of **microbes** and certain minibeasts.

Millions of Microbes

Without any minibeasts at all, compost heaps will rot thanks to millions of tiny microbes—**bacteria**, **algae**, and **fungi**. They eat dead plant and vegetable waste. The warmer the heap gets, the more they multiply.

◀ This photo shows the different stages an apple goes through as it rots. Tiny microbes on the apple slowly eat it, making it rot.

Here Come the Minibeasts!

A heap of slowly rotting material is very attractive to certain minibeasts. Some crawl in, others fly in, and some hatch from eggs laid in the compost heap.

Nature's Recyclers

Minibeasts eat the contents of the compost heap, breaking it down into smaller and smaller pieces. Along with the microbes, the minibeasts help to recycle the nutrients locked up inside the dead plant material by passing it back into the compost.

▶ A compost heap is a giant pile of food for, and waste from, minibeasts.

What's in the Heap?

The animals you will find in a compost heap depend on what kind of heap it is. If the bin has a lid and is in a sunny place, the compost grows warm as microbes do their work. The microbes will like it, but minibeasts may find it too warm. If the heap or bin is without a lid, you are more likely to find a range of different minibeasts.

◀ The minibeasts found in compost heaps eat plant material everywhere—not just in compost heaps.

Flies above the Heap

A compost heap in summer can attract a cloud of tiny fruit flies.

H Fruit flies can grow up to ¹⁄₁₆ inch (0.2 cm) long.

▲ Fruit flies have red eyes and one pair of wings.

A Good Place to Lay

The top layer of the compost heap is a good place for fruit flies to lay their eggs. These hatch into tiny **maggots**, or **larvae**, which feed on the vegetable and fruit scraps. After a few days, the maggots become **pupae**. Inside the pupae, the maggots change into adult flies.

H Fruit fly maggots can grow up to ¼ inch (0.6 cm) long.

▲ Fruit fly maggots feed on a peach. They speed up the rotting process.

Soaking Up Food

The adult fruit fly and other types of fly also feed on fruit. They eat liquid food by using their special mouth to soak up the fruit's juice, like a sponge.

If you find flies unpleasant, it is possible to stop them from living on a compost heap. If you place a layer of drier material on top of fruit or vegetable scraps, this stops the flies from laying eggs. Placing a lid on a compost bin does the same thing.

▼ This close-up photo shows a housefly feeding on a pear.

⊢⊣ Houseflies can grow up to ⁵⁄₁₆ inch (0.8 cm) long.

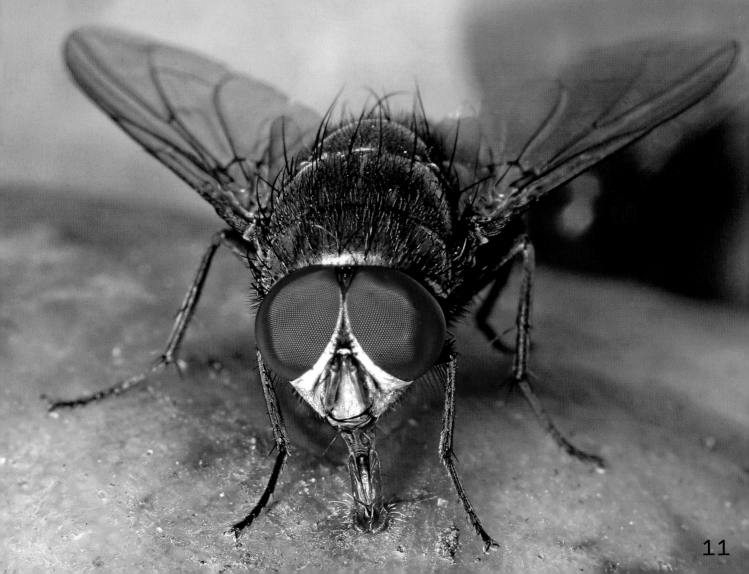

11

Slugs and Snails

Slugs and snails often find their way to a compost heap in search of food.

▶ A snail rests on a potted plant next to a compost heap.

This snail's shell can grow up to 1.5 inches (4 cm) across.

▲ Slugs help to break down plant material in gardens and open spaces.

This yellow slug can grow up to 4 inches (10 cm) long.

Helpful Mollusks

Slugs and snails belong to a group of animals called **mollusks**. Although they like to eat living plants, they also eat dead plant material lying on the ground or in the compost heap.

Damp and Slimy

Slugs and snails need to stay damp to stay alive. **Glands** on their skin make slime to help stop them from drying out. If the weather becomes too dry, they bury into soil or compost to survive.

▼ The slime also helps slugs and snails to move across the ground or up a plant.

TOP TIP!

As well as in compost heaps, look for slugs and snails resting under plant pots, stones, and among climbing plants.

The Tentacles

On the head of a slug or snail there are two pairs of **tentacles**. The long pair has black dots on the end —the eyes. Both sets of tentacles give the slug or snail its senses—sight, touch, taste, and smell.

◀ Slugs and snails have a breathing hole on the right side of the body.

13

Minibeast Hunters

Some animals are attracted to compost heaps in search of minibeasts to eat.

▶ A spider web clings to garden plants.

This wolf spider can grow up to ⅜ inch (1 cm) long.

▲ A spider injects its **prey**, a fruit fly, with poison from its fangs.

Hunting Spiders

Open compost heaps, rather than compost bins, are a good hunting ground for spiders. Some types of spider spin webs across the rotting material or on plants close by. Minibeasts get stuck in the web and the spider eats them. Other types of spiders hunt minibeasts on the compost heap or across the ground.

TOP TIP!

Some types of beetle also hunt for minibeasts in compost. Learn more about them on pages 20 and 21.

The Speedy Centipede

Centipedes eat minibeasts such as beetles, worms, and woodlice. There are plenty of these in compost, so centipedes come to compost heaps to hunt. Sometimes they live inside the heap.

▼ A centipede has one pair of legs on each **segment** of its body.

This centipede can grow up to 1.4 inches (3.5 cm) long.

There are two main types of centipedes—the ones that live under stones and the ones that live in soil or compost. Their name means "a hundred legs" but the common centipede has only 30 legs, while others have more than 100 legs.

▼ Compost heaps provide easy meals for birds.

Larger Visitors

Birds, hedgehogs, and toads visit the compost heap to eat worms and other minibeasts. Hedgehogs, toads, and grass snakes may even crawl into the center of a heap to **hibernate** as it is a warm, safe place to rest.

Woodlice, Millipedes, and Earwigs

Take the lid off a compost bin or stir up the top layer and you will probably see woodlice and maybe millipedes running for cover.

◀ Woodlice use their **antennas** to find their way in the dark compost.

▼ The shiny shell of a woodlouse is made up of sections joined together like armor.

├──────┤ This woodlouse can grow up to ⅜ inch (1.1 cm) long.

Dark and Damp

Both woodlice and millipedes like to live in a dark, damp habitat. They eat rotting wood and leaves and are helpful to us all. They break down dead plant material in and out of the compost heap.

TOP TIP!

If you don't have a compost heap, you could look for woodlice and millipedes under stones, potted plants, or logs.

Millipedes

Millipedes, like centipedes, have long, slim bodies and lots of legs. They come to the compost heap to eat dead plant material. They move more slowly than centipedes.

▶ Some types of millipede curl up to rest, or to protect themselves from **predators**.

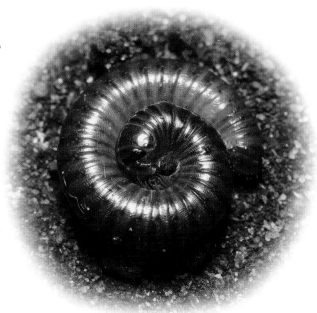

This millipede can grow up to 2.3 inches (6 cm) long.

Earwigs

Earwigs usually live in cracks, under stones or in other dark places. These **nocturnal** minibeasts look for dead plant material to eat and so may visit compost heaps.

◀ Earwigs have long antennas on the head and **pincers** at the tail end.

This earwig can grow up to ½ inch (1.3 cm) long.

Tunneling Worms

Worms find their way into a compost heap from under the ground. Soon they make the heap into their home.

▲ Worms can eat half their own body weight in compost every day.

Lots of Worms

There are several different types of worms. The ones that like to live in compost heaps also live in the top layer of soil. All worms are long, slim minibeasts and are a pale pink or reddish color.

▼ The tiger worm gets its name because it has stripes on its body.

This tiger worm can grow up to 4 inches (10 cm) long.

TOP TIP!

If you want to watch worms at work, place a handful of damp compost, including worms, in a glass jar with a lid. Make a few air holes in the lid and watch the worms at work. Remember to return the worms to the heap after a day.

Important Work

Worms push themselves through compost, eating dead plant material. It goes through their body and comes out as a fine-grained, dark waste. Worms make tunnels through the compost, allowing air to get into the heap. This helps the microbes to live and breed.

▲ Worms mix up all the layers of compost.

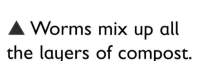
Ants sometimes make their nest, called a colony, in a dry compost heap. You may see an ant visiting a compost heap to collect tiny bits of fruit for the colony.

Beetles and Compost

Beetles visit compost heaps in search of food. While some types of beetles eat dead plant material, many are looking for smaller minibeasts to hunt and eat.

▲ This ground beetle eats minibeasts but also likes to feed on bits of fruit in the compost heap.

Ground Beetles

Ground beetles like to rest under stones, logs, or in leaf litter. However, when they feel hungry, some find their way to the compost heap for a feast. They eat other minibeasts including worms, woodlice, slugs, and snails.

▼ The ground beetle's strong jaws pull a snail out of its shell and crunch it up.

This violet ground beetle can grow up to 1.2 inches (3 cm) long.

Grubs

If a compost heap does not get disturbed too often, you may find beetle **grubs**. These fat, white creatures have six legs and they eat the dead plant material in the heap. After some months, the grubs turn into pupae and then into adult beetles.

▲ The rose chafer grub stays in compost or under the ground for several months.

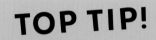

TOP TIP!

Look out for beetle grubs in rotting wood or under soil. Many types of beetle lay their eggs in rotting wood, under the bark of trees or in soil.

▼ You may see a beautiful rose chafer beetle crawling out of your compost heap.

This rose chafer beetle can grow up to ¾ inch (1.7 cm) long.

A Handful of Compost

Some of the minibeasts that live in compost are tiny. Follow this activity to see what you can find.

You will need:
- Disposable gloves • Compost from a heap • A pale tray or sheet of white paper • A fine paintbrush • A magnifying glass • Plastic or glass jars • A pencil and paper

What to do:
- With your gloves on, take a handful of compost and spread it thinly on the paper or tray.

- Use the paintbrush to gently move things about.

- Use a magnifying glass and look at the identification guide on pages 26–27 to help name the minibeasts you find.

- Carefully put some of the animals in the jars for a closer look. Draw some of the minibeasts that you find.

- Remember to put the minibeasts back where you found them.

⚠️ Wash your hands after you have handled compost or soil.

Along with the other minibeasts in this book, you might see these tiny minibeasts with a magnifying glass or a microscope.

▶ Pseudoscorpion: It hunts through compost for other smaller minibeasts, such as mites (see below), to eat. Its long pincers pierce and poison its prey but are harmless to us.

This pseudoscorpion can grow up to ⅛ inch (0.3 cm) long.

◀ Mites: There are masses of mites in compost. Most eat rotting plant material but some types are predators, eating other tiny animals including other mites.

This red velvet mite is one of the biggest types of mites and can grow up to ⅛ inch (0.3 cm) long.

▶ Springtail: This insect has no wings, but it does have a special spring underneath its body that allows it to jump.

This springtail can grow up to ³⁄₁₆ inch (0.5 cm) long.

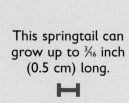

23

Make Your Own Compost

It is easy to make compost if you follow these instructions. You do have to be patient, as it can take several months for rotting material to become compost.

What to do:

• Find a good site where the heap or bin can be left undisturbed. It is best if it is away from the house or school building and on grass or soil.

• Decide whether you are going to make a compost heap, build a compost bin, or buy one.

• Start collecting material for the heap—see the box opposite for suggestions.

• Add these to the compost heap or bin. You may need to add some water to keep it all damp.

• If there is a lid, use it.

- After several months, you will start to see fine, dark material at the bottom of the heap. Use it around the garden.

- Remember to look for minibeasts to study in your compost heap.

▶ You could make a simple heap like this one . . .

▼ . . . or buy a plastic compost bin like this one . . .

▼ . . . or ask an adult to build a compost bin like this one.

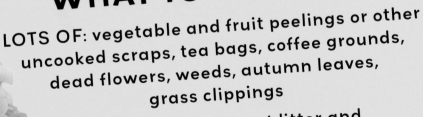

WHAT TO COMPOST

LOTS OF: vegetable and fruit peelings or other uncooked scraps, tea bags, coffee grounds, dead flowers, weeds, autumn leaves, grass clippings

SOME: egg shells, pet litter and straw/hay (from hamster, rabbit, or guinea pig cages only), newspaper or cardboard, and twigs (cut up as small as possible)

NO: cooked food, meat, dog or cat litter, plastic or glass

Identification Guide

Use this guide to help you identify the minibeasts that you find. They are listed in the order in which they are featured in the book. There are thousands of different minibeasts, so you may need to use a field guide or the Internet, too.

Fly: There are thousands of different types of flies. They are all flying insects with one pair of wings. Use a field guide to identify the type.

Fly maggot: The wriggling, legless larva of a fly is often found in big groups, feeding on rotting material.

Slug: A mollusk, the slug has a shiny, wet body and moves along on its one "foot."

Snail: The snail carries its shell on its soft body and is a mollusk, like the slug.

Spider: Spiders are a type of **arachnid**, a group of animals that includes harvestmen, scorpions, the tiny pseudoscorpions, and mites. Spiders all have eight legs and two parts—the head and the abdomen (body).

Centipede: A long, slim minibeast with several pairs of legs. It is a predator, eating other minibeasts including centipedes.

Woodlouse: A woodlouse is a type of **crustacean**, a group of animals that includes shrimps and crabs. There are many different types of woodlice, but most are grey with shiny, hard skins. A woodlouse has 14 legs and is nocturnal, resting during the day.

Millipede: A millipede is long and slim and moves fairly slowly on its many legs. There are three main types: snake millipedes, pill millipedes, and flat-backed millipedes.

Earwig: A small, brown, shiny insect with pincers at the back of its body. It usually lives under stones or in cracks in the wall or ground.

Worm: A long, pale-colored minibeast that spends most of its life tunneling underground or through compost heaps. The long body is divided into segments. The head is at the front of a moving worm.

Ant: A small, six-legged insect with long antennas. It spends most of its life collecting food and taking it back to its colony —the group of ants it lives with.

Beetle: Beetles are insects and they have two pairs of wings. One of these sets of wings is hard and protects the soft set underneath.

Beetle grub: The young of a beetle, also called a larva. Some grubs live underground, others live in rotting wood.

Pseudoscorpion: A tiny arachnid, the pseudoscorpion has large pincers at the front of its body.

Mite: This tiny animal has eight legs and is an arachnid, like the spider. Millions of mites live in soil and compost heaps.

Springtail: This tiny insect is about the size of a pin head. It has a special spring under the tail that allows it to jump.

Glossary

Alga (plural algae) A very tiny and simple plant.

Animals The huge group of living things including birds, insects, mammals, crustaceans, reptiles, and amphibians.

Antennas Feelers on an insect's head and used for smell, taste, and touch.

Arachnid An animal with eight legs, like a spider, pseudoscorpion, or mite.

Backbone The line of bones down the middle of the skeleton.

Bacterium (plural bacteria) A very small living thing that lives in soil, water, air, and inside our bodies. Some bacteria cause diseases.

Crustaceans A large group of animals, including woodlice. Most of the others, such as crabs, lobsters, and shrimp, live in the sea.

Fungus (plural fungi) A type of plant, without leaves, that feeds on rotting material.

Gland In slugs and snails a tiny body part that produces slime.

Grub The larva of a beetle.

Habitat A place where certain plants and animals like to live.

Hibernate To spend the winter in a deep state of sleep.

Insects A huge group of animals. All insects have a body in three parts: the head at one end, thorax in the middle, and abdomen at the other end. Six legs are attached to the thorax and many insects also have wings.

Invertebrates A huge group of animals without a backbone including insects, worms, and spiders.

Larva (plural larvae) The stage in the **life cycle** of many insects after they hatch from eggs.

Life Cycle The lifetime of a living thing, from birth until death. An insect life cycle often goes through these stages: egg, larva, pupa, and adult.

Maggots Another name for the larvae of some insects, usually flies.

Microbe A tiny living thing that can usually be seen only by using a microscope. Microbes include bacteria, algae, and fungi.

Molluscs A large group of animals with soft bodies. Slugs, snails, octopuses, mussels, and oysters are all molluscs.

Nocturnal Animals that rest during the day and are active at night.

Pincer A claw used to grab things.

Predators Animals that hunt other animals for food, rather than eating plants.

Prey Animals that other animals hunt to eat.

Pupa (plural pupae) Part of the life cycle of many insects before they turn into adults.

Rot The natural process that breaks down materials.

Segment A part or section of something.

Tentacles On a snail or slug, springy threads on the head used to help the animal feel or see its way around.

Web Sites to Visit

http://sustainable.tamu.edu/slidesets/kidscompost/cover.html
A slide show of how kids can make a compost bin.

www.bbc.co.uk/nature/reallywild/amazing
This BBC site contains facts about many amazing animals, including woodlice, slugs, and leaf-cutter ants.

Note to Parents and Teachers:
Every effort has been made by the publishers to ensure that these web sites are suitable for children, that they are of the highest educational value, and that they contain no inappropriate or offensive material. However, because of the nature of the Internet, it is impossible to guarantee that the contents of these sites will not be altered. We strongly advise that Internet access is supervised by a responsible adult.

Index